Billie Eilish

Biography, Facts & Quotes

--Tom Cannon

Book 1 Of Series "I Love My Celeb"

Book Contents

Biography of Billie Eilish

Billie Eilish – Childhood & Early Life

Billie Eilish – Career

Billie Eilish – Personal Life

Billie Eilish – Quotes for Your Instagram Caption

I Love Billie Eilish

Biography Of Billie Eilish

Billie Eilish is on the rise. She is an American singer and songwriter and the current heart throb of teens. Billie is known for her successful debut single "Ocean

Eyes". Billie Eilish belongs to a family of musicians and was born and raised in Los Angeles, California. Coming from a family of musicians, she is destined to become the queen of singing. Her performing arts career is sky-rocketing because she is super talented and super relatable. At age 8, Billie Eilish joined a choir, she started writing and singing her own songs by the time she turned 11.

Billie Eilish loves her elder brother Finneas O'Connell and he is the biggest influence in her life and music career. Billie's elder brother had his own band. He had written a song titled "Ocean Eyes'. Our queen Billie performed the song and released it online on an audio distribution platform SoundCloud. Guess whaaat! It became a massive success. Ocean Blues turned out to be Billie's first and huge breakthrough. In 2017, Billie's brother Finneas helped her record the single "Bellyache" and it too became a huge hit.

Continuing the success of Bellyache, in August 2017, Billie released her debut EP, "Don't Smile At Me". The EP appeared on several American and international music charts and reached the Top 15 in the United Stated, United Kingdom, Canada and Australia.

Following her EP's success, in October 2017 Apple named her their newest 'UP NEXT" artist.

In April 2018, the single "Lovely" was released which was Billie Eilish's collaboration with American singer Khalid. The single "Lovely" was added to the soundtrack for the second season of 13 Reasons Why.

On March 29, 2019, Billie Eilish's debut studio album "When We All Fall Asleep, Where Do We Go?" was released. It received widespread critical acclaim from celebrities in the performing arts industry and loved by fans across the world.

"When We All Fall Asleep, Where Do We Go?" reached number one in the United States, United Kingdom, Canada and Australia. Its singles "When the Party's Over", "Bury a Friend" and "Bad Guy" all reached the top 15 in the United States, the latter reaching number one in Canada and Australia. Eilish has seven gold and two platinum singles through RIAA.

Billie Eilish

Childhood & Early Life

Billie Eilish was born Billie Eilish Pirate Baird O'Connell, on December 18, 2001, in Los Angeles, California. She was born into a family of musicians and actors. She grew up with her elder brother. Her parents, Maggie Baird and Patrick O'Connell, were popular figures in the American entertainment industry.

While growing up, she saw her elder brother, Finneas O'Connell, fall in love with music. Additionally, her mother wrote songs and her father played instruments such as the piano and the ukulele. The musical vibe in the house inspired little Billie to make a career in music.

She grew up listening to the music of 'The Beatles' and Avril Lavigne. Her father loved making mixtapes of various artists.

She was home-schooled for most of her early years, but that did not stop her from participating in extracurricular activities. She loved acting in homemade films and also sang and danced whenever she found the chance.

When she turned 8 years old, she joined a choir and sang with them for three years. By the time she was 11 years old, she was already writing and composing songs of her own. She also made several short films. She shot them on a camera and edited them on 'iMovie,' 'Apple's video-editing app.

Other than acting and music, dance was another passion of hers. She took dance classes in her early teenage years. With a plethora of skills, she aimed at making a big career in the show business.

Her elder brother had a band of his own. He had written a song named 'Ocean Eyes' and asked his sister to record it in her voice. This accidental song turned out to be the breakthrough success for Billie and boosted her career.

Billie Eilish

Career

The song 'Ocean Eyes' was recorded in October 2015. It was initially meant for Billie's dance classes. She handed over the song to her dance teacher and meant it to be featured in her next dance routine. The song turned out to be good, and the siblings decided that it must be up on the music-sharing platform 'SoundCloud.'

The song was uploaded on 'SoundCloud' in early 2016, and by March, the music video was released. The song shot up and registered more than 10 million hits within a short period of time. This success was unexpected and made way for many more versions. In November 2016, a music video with Billie dancing on the song was released. It turned out to be another success.

Several major record labels came ahead to buy the rights for the song. The song was released worldwide by 'Darkroom' and' Interscope Records.' It immediately became a critical and commercial success. Toward the end of the year, Billie released another single, 'Six Feet Under.'

Inspired by the success of her debut single, 'Ocean Eyes,' Billie recorded four remixes of the song and compiled them all in an EP titled 'Ocean Eyes.' All the remixes became big hits and gave Billie enough courage to carry on with her future projects.

In February 2017, Billie released the single, 'Bellyache,' which was produced and co-written by her brother. The music video for the song, directed by Miles and AJ, was released in March 2017.

Billie then recorded a song titled 'Bored,' which was included in the official soundtrack of the famous 'Netflix' series '13 Reasons Why.' Two more singles, 'Watch' and 'Copycat,' were subsequently released. In July 2017, Billie announced her highly awaited debut EP, 'Don't Smile at Me.'

Before the official release of the EP, she released two singles from the same, 'My Boy' and 'Idontwannabeyouanymore.' Leading up to the release of the EP, she added new songs every Friday. The EP was eventually released on August 12, 2017.

The same year, she collaborated with Vince Staples and released a remix of her song 'Watch,' which was renamed '&Burn.' In order to promote herself more, she embarked on a tour in January 2018. The tour ended in August 2018.

She also collaborated with famous American singer Khalid and worked with him on a single titled 'Lovely,' which was released in mid-2018. The song became immensely popular and made the producers of '13 Reasons Why' buy its rights and feature it in the second season of the series.

In 2018, she released the singles 'Bitches Broken Hearts,' and 'You Should See me in a Crown.' On March 29, 2019, Billie Eilish's debut studio album "When We All Fall Asleep, Where Do We Go?" was released and received worldwide critical acclaim.

Billie Eilish

Personal Life

Billie Eilish has been criticized for never smiling in photographs. She has responded to such criticism by saying that she does not like smiling because it makes her feel weak and powerless.

She is known for her eccentric dress sense. She is often criticized for it but does not pay attention to the criticism.

"Let me let you go" - when the party's over

"You and I are suicidal stolen art." - bitches broken hearts

"Tore my shirt to stop you bleedin'." - when the party's over

"Was I made from a broken mold?" - idontwannabeyouanymore

"I guess being lonely fits me." - bitches broken hearts

"Help, I lost myself again." - six feet under

When you are feeling yourself

"You can pretend you don't miss me." - bitches broken hearts

"I wanna make 'em scared like I could be anywhere." - bellyache

"Wait 'til the world is mine." - you should see me in a crown

"All you wanna do is kiss me, oh what a shame I'm not there." bitches broken hearts

"My V is for Vendetta." - bellyache

"You should see me in a crown." - you should see me in a crown

"You committed, I'm your crime." - COPYCAT

"I'm gonna run this nothing town." - you should see me in a crown

"Your trigger finger's mine." - COPYCAT

"Watch me make 'em bow one by one." - you should see me in a crown

"I don't belong to anyone, but everybody knows my name." - COPYCAT

"Your silence is my favorite sound." - you should see me in a crown

"Why so sad, bunny, can't have mine?" - COPYCAT

"I'm not your baby." - you should see me in a crown

"You're italic, I'm in bold." - COPYCAT

"I'm sorry...sike." – COPYCAT

When you're happy

"Wake up and smell the coffee." - come out and play

"Dreaming of a time and place." - WHEN I WAS OLDER

"You'll never know until you try it." - come out and play

"Look up, out of your window." come out and play

When you're crushing hard on someone

"I wanna be alone...alone with you, does that make sense?" - hostage

"I hope you stay." - come out and play

"You feel right, so stay a sec." - hostage

"You don't have to keep it quiet." - come out and play

"This feels right, so stay a sec." - hostage

"I've been watching you for some time." - ocean eyes

"Kiss me until I can't speak." - hostage

"Falling into your ocean eyes." - ocean eyes

"Let me crawl inside your veins." - hostage

"I've never fallen from quite this high." - ocean eyes

"Can't stop thinking of your diamond mind." - ocean eyes

When you're having boy / girl trouble

"My boy don't love me like he promised." - my boy

"You really know how to make me cry." - ocean eyes

"Don't come back, it won't end well." - six feet under

"The games you played were never fun." - bored

"If we were meant to be, we would have been by now." - watch

"You just want what you can't have." - party favor

"My boy's an ugly crier but he's such a pretty liar." - my boy

"Our love is six feet under." - six feet under

"I just want you to set me free." - bored

"I'll never let you back to put it out." - watch

"I'm not your party favor." - party favor

"You want me to be yours, well then you gotta be mine." - my boy

"Erase your touch." - six feet under

"You'd say you'd stay but then you'd run." - bored

"Your love feels so fake." - watch

"We can't change the weather." - party favor

"If you want a good girl, then goodbye." - my boy

"You're cold as a knife." - six feet under

"What makes you sure you're all I need?" - bored

"When you call my name, do you think I'll come runnin'?" - watch

"I hope you don't think that shit's fair." - bored

"Let you burn." - watch

"Can't you see that I'm getting bored?" - bored

"And when you walk out the door and leave me torn, you're teaching me to live without it." – bored

I Love Billie Eilish

Review Request

If you loved this book, please leave an honest review on amazon

For More Books On "I Love My Celeb" Series

Follow Author "Tom Cannon" on Amazon

Made in the USA
Columbia, SC
26 November 2019